Tail Lights

&

Tail Wags

Dogs aren't easy.

They can make you laugh, and they can make you cry.

They can drive you crazy, then comfort you when you've gone completely 'round the bend.

They make you wonder why you ever brought them home, but you miss them like crazy anytime they're not with you.

They create a colossal mess, then watch you while you clean it up (usually from just around a corner).

Yep. They're really not easy, but you'll never know a deeper, more devoted love than what your dog has for you.

There she goes.

I think she'll come back for us.

Maybe not.

Humph.

She didn't turn around.

Guess we'll just wait here.

Sigh.

> Hmm. It's been awhile. How about the loveseat? She'll still be happy.

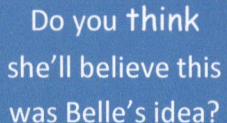
Do you think she'll believe this was Belle's idea?

> I really had to go out.
>
> Belle did too, and the door fell down!
>
> We both sit really well, don't you think?

She's HOME!

She's quiet and kinda stiff looking.

Uh oh!

We're going outside now it seems.

That's good, right?

Yeah.

She still loves us.

Maybe we can go along next time.

It's been a very long day. Maybe tomorrow we can go too!

Dreaming of going with her for a day of fun.

Sun's up!

She's still asleep.

No work today?

Oh boy!

It takes Belle awhile to understand what's going on, but when she figures it out . . .

She goes a little crazy!

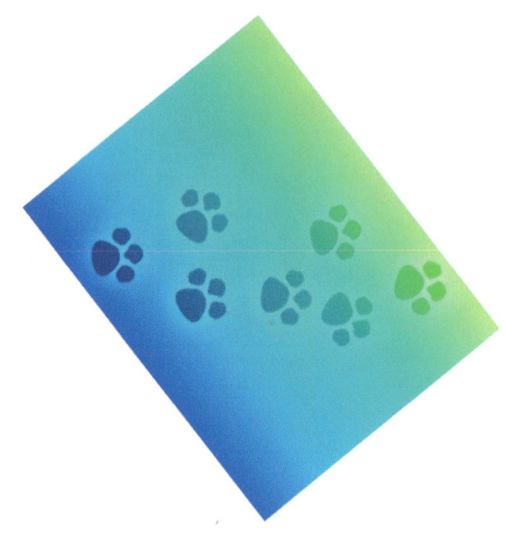

Funny story!

One time, Mama A left her car door open. I jumped in and pretended I was going to drive! Guess who gave in and took me for a ride?

Did you ever *go* to a party?

I go to parties, and I let Belle come too! They're lots of fun!

Woo woo woo!

I went to a **reunion** party. I met new **people**.

I was silly and made a little girl named Katie laugh!

I was helpful and took **berries** off a bush with Mama A and Pap.

I was strong and kind when a nice lady named Aunt Eleanor needed me.

> I went to a birthday party for my Nana too!
>
> I made new friends and started out on my best behavior . . .

Until there was . . .

PAPER!!!

We had lots of fun, and then we had to rest inside while the people had birthday cake outside.

Pap is the best at cuddle time.

> I know all about Christmas.
> It's a party, kind of . . .

A tree came in the house, but no one noticed it. I tried not to look at it and stayed close to Pap. He's a little guy, but he always makes me feel safe.

Mama J told me a story about a star, a baby, and three kings. It was a nice story. I liked it.

There's some crazy stuff about Christmas too!

But I figured out it's mostly about family . . .

Bet it's because of the family in the Christmas story.

Don't you think so too?

Sometimes we wear clothes.

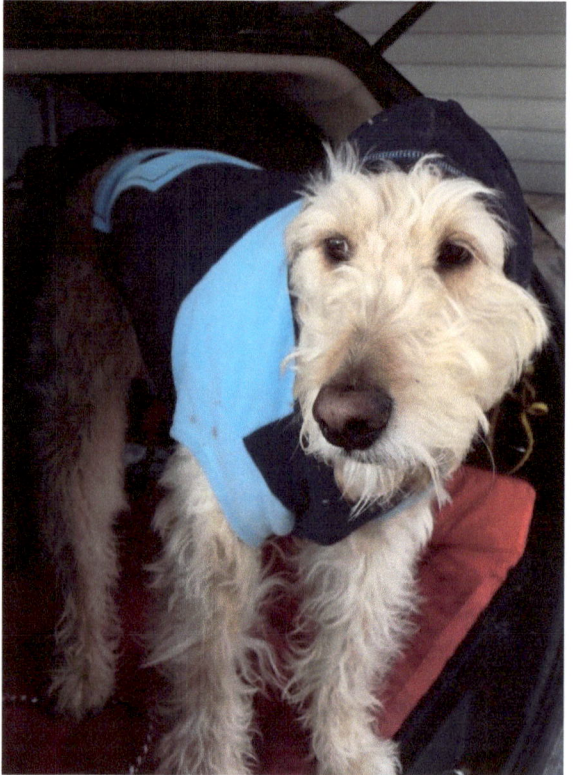

I've been lots of places!

Do you know where my favorite place is?

It's my HOME!!!

I love my deck!

I love my hammock!

One time, this tiny person came to visit me at my home. I stayed very close and very calm.

His name was Patrick!

Mama A got to hold him for a little while. I hung out with the big guy till he took the little person back.

I showed Patrick around my neighborhood.

Patrick gets bigger every time he visits! I can walk him now.

I love my Patrick!

He's my best friend!

When my Nana and Pap come to visit, I love on them like no one else! They really love me (and Belle too)!

Katie was a great guest! She shared her snacks with me!

My mamas love me!

www.ingramcontent.com/pod-product-compliance
Lightning Source LLC
Chambersburg PA
CBHW041523220426
43669CB00002B/29